三字经

Three Character Classic

Written by Wang Yinglin 王應麟
1223-1296

Chinese/English Side-by-Side

DRAGON READER

Translation by Herbert Giles (1845-1935)

Cover Design © Copyright 2016 Dragon Reader

人之初　性本善　性相近　习相远
性乃迁　教之道　贵以专　昔孟母　择邻处
子不学　断机杼　窦燕山　有义方　教五子
名俱扬　养不教　父之过　教不严　师之惰
子不学　非所宜　幼不学　老何为　王不琢
不成器　人不学　不知义　为人子　方少时
亲师友　习礼仪　香九龄　能温席　孝于亲
所当执　融四岁　能让梨　弟于长　宜先知
首孝弟　次见闻　知某数　识某文　一而十
十而百　百而千　千而万　三才者　天地人
三光者　日月星　三纲者　君臣义　父子亲
夫妇顺　曰春夏　曰秋冬　此四时　运不穷
曰南北　曰西东　此四方
木金土　此五行　本乎数　十干者　甲至癸
十二支　子至亥　曰黄道　日所躔　曰赤道

Table of Contents

1-5 人之初

人之初，性本善。性相近，習相遠。

Men at their birth

are naturally good.

Their natures are much the same;

their habits become widely different.

苟不教，性乃遷。教之道，貴以專。

If foolishly there is no teaching,

the nature will deteriorate.

The right way in teaching

is to attach the utmost importance in thoroughness.

昔孟母，擇鄰處。子不學，斷機杼。

Of old, the mother of Mencius

chose a neighbourhood;

and when her child would not learn,

she broke the shuttle from the loom.

竇燕山，有義方。教五子，名俱揚。

Dou of the Swallow Hills

had the right method.

He taught five sons,

each of whom raised the family reputation.

養不教，父之過。教不嚴，師之惰。

To feed without teaching

is the father's fault.

To teach without severity

is the teacher's laziness.

6-10 子不學

子不學，非所宜。幼不學，老何為。

If the child does not learn,

this is not as it should be.

If he does not learn while young,

what will he be when old?

玉不琢，不成器。人不學，不知義。

If jade is not polished,

it cannot become a thing of use.

If a man does not learn,

he cannot know his duty towards his neighbour.

為人子，方少時。親師友，習禮儀。

He who is the son of a man,

when he is young

should attach himself to his teachers and friends,

and practise ceremonial usages.

香九齡，能溫席。孝於親，所當執。

Xiang, at nine years of age,

could warm (his parents') bed.

Filial piety towards parents,

is that to which we should hold fast.

融四歲，能讓梨。弟於長，宜先知。

Rong, at four years of age,

could yield the (bigger) pears.

To behave as a younger brother towards elders,

is one of the first things to know.

11-15 首孝弟

首孝弟，次見聞。知某數，識某文。

Begin with filial piety and fraternal love,

and then see and hear.

Learn to count,

and learn to read.

一而十，十而百。百而千，千而萬。

Units and tens,

tens and hundreds,

hundreds and thousands,

thousands and tens of thousands.

三才者，天地人。三光者，日月星。

The Three Forces

are Heaven, Earth and Man.

The Three Luminaries

are the sun, the moon and the stars.

三綱者，君臣義。父子親，夫婦順。

The Three Bonds

are the obligation between sovereign and subject,

the love between father and child,

the harmony between husband and wife.

曰春夏，曰秋冬。此四時，運不窮。

We speak of spring and summer,

we speak of autumn and winter.

These four seasons

revolve without ceasing.

16-20 曰南北

曰南北，曰西東。此四方，應乎中。

We speak of North and South,

we speak of East and West,

These four points

respond to the requirements of the centre.

曰水火，木金土。此五行，本乎數。

We speak of water, fire,

wood, metal and earth.

These five elements

have their origin in number.

曰仁義，禮智信。此五常，不容紊。

We speak of charity of heart and of duty towards one's neighbour,

of propriety, of wisdom, and of truth.

These five virtues

admit of no compromise.

稻粱菽，麥黍稷。此六谷，人所食。

Rice, spiked millet, pulse,

wheat, glutinous millet and common millet.

These six grains

are those which men eat.

馬牛羊，雞犬豕。此六畜，人所飼。

The horse, the ox, the sheep,

the fowl, the dog, the pig.

These six animals,

are those which men keep.

21-25 曰喜怒

曰喜怒，曰哀懼。愛惡欲，七情具。

We speak of joy, of anger,

we speak of pity, of fear,

of love, of hate, and of desire.

These are the seven passions.

匏土革，木石金。與絲竹，乃八音。

The gourd, earthenware, skin,

wood, stone, metal,

silk, and bamboo,

yield the eight musical sounds.

高曾祖，父而身。身而子，子而孫。自子孫，至玄（1）曾。乃九族，人之倫。

Great great grandfather, great grandfather, grandfather,

father and self,

self and son,

son and grandson,

from son and grandson

on to great grandson and great great grandson.

These are the nine agnates,

constituting the kinships of man.

（1.） 玄 : Originally read: "元". 避諱。

父子恩，夫婦從。兄則友，弟則恭。長幼
序，友與朋。君則敬，臣則忠。此十義，
人所同。

Affection between father and child,

harmony between husband and wife,

friendliness on the part of elder brothers,

respectfulness on the part of younger brothers,

precedence between elders and youngers,

as between friend and friend,

respect on the part of the sovereign,

loyalty on the part of the subject.

These ten obligations,

are common to all men.

凡訓蒙，須講究。詳訓詁，名句讀。

In the education of the young,

there should be explanation and elucidation,

careful teaching of the interpretations of commentators,

and due attention to paragraphs and sentences.

26-30 為學者

為學者，必有初。小學終，至四書。

Those who are learners,

must have a beginning.

The "little learning" finished,

they proceed to the four books.

論語者，二十篇。群弟子，記善言。

There is the Lun Yu,

in twenty sections.

In this, the various disciples

have recorded the wise sayings of Confucius.

孟子者，七篇止。講道德，說仁義。

The works of Mencius

are comprised in seven sections.

These explain the way and the exemplification thereof,

and expound charity and duty towards one's neighbour.

作中庸，子思筆。中不偏，庸不易。

The Zhong Yong was written

by the pen of Zi-si;

Zhong (the middle) being that which does not lean towards any side,

Yong (the course) being that which cannot be changed.

作大學，乃曾子。自修齊，至平治。

He who wrote The Great Learning

was the philosopher Zeng.

Beginning with cultivation of the individual and ordering of the family,

it goes on to government of one's own State and ordering of the Empire.

31-35 孝經通

孝經通，四書熟。如六經，始可讀。

When the Classic of Filial Piety is mastered,

and the "Four books" are known by heart,

the next step is to the "Six classics",

which may now be studied.

詩書易，禮春秋。號六經，當講求。

The Books of Poetry, of History and of Changes.

The Rites of the Zhou Dynasty, the Book of Rites, and the Spring and Autumn Annals,

are called the Six Classics,

which should be carefully explained and analysed.

有連山，有歸藏。有周易，三易詳。

There is the Lian Shan system,

there is the Gui Zang,

And there is the system of Changes of the Zhou Dynasty;

such are the three systems which elucidate the Changes.

有典謨，有訓誥。有誓命，書之奧。

There are the Regulations, the Counsels,

the Instructions, the Announcements,

the Oaths, the Charges;

these are the profundities of the Book of History.

我周公，作周禮。著六官，存治體。

Our Duke of Zhou

drew up the Ritual of the Zhou Dynasty,

in which he set forth the duties of the six classes of officials;

and thus gave a settled form to the government.

36-40 大小戴

大小戴，註禮記。述聖言，禮樂備。

The Elder and the Younger Dai

wrote commentaries on the Book of Rites.

They published the holy words,

and Ceremonies and Music were set in order.

曰國風，曰雅頌。號四詩，當諷詠。

We speak of the Guo Feng,

we speak of the Ya and the Song.

These are the four sections of the Book of poetry,

which should be hummed over and over.

詩既亡，春秋作。寓褒貶，別善惡。

When odes ceased to be made,

the Spring and Autumn Annals were produced.

These Annals contain praise and blame,

and distinguish the good from the bad.

三傳者，有公羊。有左氏，有穀梁。

The three commentaries upon the above

include that of Gong-Yang,

that of Zuo

and that of Gu-Liang.

經既明，方讀子。撮其要，記其事。

When the Classics are understood,

then the writings of the various philosophers should be read.

Pick out the important points in each,

and take a note of all facts.

41-45 五子者

五子者，有荀楊。文中子，及老莊。

The five chief philosophers

are Xun, Yang,

Wenzhongzi,

Laozi and Zhuangzi.

經子通，讀諸史。考世系，知終始。

When the Classics and the Philosophers
are mastered,

the various histories should be read,

and the genealogical connections should
be examined,

so that the end of one dynasty and the
beginning of the next may be known.

自羲農，至黃帝。號三皇，居上世。

From Fu Xi and Shen Nong

on to the Yellow Emperor,

these are called the Three Rulers.

who lived in the early ages.

唐有虞，號二帝。相揖遜，稱盛世。

Tang and You-Yu

are called the two emperors.

They adbicated, one after the other,

and theirs was called the Golden Age.

夏有禹，商有湯。周文王，稱三王。

The Xia dynasty has Yu;

the Shang dynasty has Tang;

the Zhou dynasty had Wen and Wu;

these are called the Three Kings

46-50 夏傳子

夏傳子，家天下。四百載，遷夏社。

Under the Xia dynasty the throne was transmitted from father to son,

making a family possession of the empire.

After four hundred years,

the Imperial sacrifice passed from the House of Xia.

湯伐夏，國號商。六百載，至紂亡。

Tang the completer destroyed the Xia Dynasty,

and the dynastic title became Shang.

The line lasted for six hundred years,

ending with Zhou Xin.

周武王，始誅紂。八百載，最長久。

King Wu of the Zhou Dynasty

finally slew Zhou Xin.

His own line lasted for eight hundred years;

the longest dynasty of all.

周轍東，王綱墮。逞干戈，尚游說。

When the Zhous made tracks eastwards,

the feudal bond was slackened;

the arbitrament of spear and shields prevailed;

and peripatetic politicians were held in high esteem.

始春秋，終戰國。五霸強，七雄出。

This period began with the Spring and Autumn Epoch,

and ended with that of the Warring States.

Next, the Five Chieftains domineered,

and the Seven Martial States came to the front.

51-55 嬴秦氏

嬴秦氏，始兼並。傳二世，楚漢爭。

Then the House of Qin, descended from the Ying clan,

finally united all the states under one sway.

The thrown was transmitted to Er Shi,

upon which followed the struggle between the Chu and the Han States.

高祖興，漢業建。至孝平，王莽篡。

Then Gao Zu arose,

and the House of Han was established.

When we come to the reign of Xiao Ping,

Wang Mang usurped the throne.

光武興，為東漢。四百年，終於獻。

Then Guang Wu arose,

and founded the Eastern Han dynasty.

It lasted four hundred years,

and ended with the Emperor Xian.

魏蜀吳，爭漢鼎。號三國，迄兩晉。

Wei, Shu and Wu,

fought for the sovereignty of the Hans.

They were called the Three Kingdoms,

and existed until the Two Jin Dynasties.

宋齊繼，梁陳承。為南朝，都金陵。

Then followed the Song and the Qi dynasties,

and after them the Liang and Chen dynasties.

These are the Southern dynasties,

with their capital at Nanjing.

56-60 北元魏

北元魏，分東西。宇文周，興高齊。

The northern dynasties are the Wei dynasty of the Yuan family,

which split into Eastern and Western We,.

the Zhou dynasty of the Yuwen family,

with the Qi dynasty of the Gao family.

迨至隋，一土宇。不再傳，失統緒。

At length, under the Sui dynasty,

the empire was united under one ruler.

The throne was not transmitted twice,

succession to power being lost.

唐高祖，起義師。除隋亂，創國基。

The first emperor of the Tang dynasty

raised volunteer troops.

He put an end to the disorder of the
House of Sui,

and established the foundations of his line.

二十傳，三百載。梁滅之，國乃改。

Twenty times the thrown was transmitted

in a period of three hundred years.

The Liang State destroyed it,

and the dynastic title was changed.

梁唐晉，及漢周。稱五代，皆有由。

The Liang, the Tang, the Jin,

the Han, and the Zhou,

are called the Five Dynasties,

and there was a reason for the establishment of each.

61-65 炎宋興

炎宋興，受周禪。十八傳，南北混。

Then the fire-led house of Song arose,

and received the resignation of the house of Zhou.

Eighteen times the throne was transmitted,

and then the north and the south were reunited.

十七史，全在茲。載治亂，知興衰。

The Seventeen Dynastic Histories

are all embraced in the above.

They contain examples of good and bad government,

whence may be learnt the principles of prosperity and decay.

讀史書，考實錄。通古今，若親目。

Ye who read history

must study the State Annals,

whereby you will understand ancient and modern events,

as though having seen them with your own eyes.

口而誦，心而惟。朝於斯，夕於斯。

Recite them with the mouth,

and ponder over them in your hearts.

Do this in the morning;

do this in the evening.

昔仲尼，師項橐。古聖賢，尚勤學。

Of old, Confucius

took Xiang Tuo for his teacher.

The inspired men and sages of old

studied diligently nevertheless.

66-70 趙中令

趙中令，讀魯論。彼既仕，學且勤。

Zhao, president of the Council,

studied the Lu text of the Lun Yu.

He, when already an official,

studied, and moreover with diligence.

披蒲編，削竹簡。彼無書，且知勉。

One opened out rushes and plaited them together;

another scraped tablets of bamboo.

These men had no books,

but they knew how to make an effort.

頭懸梁，錐刺股。彼不教，自勤苦。

One tied his head to the beam above him;

another pricked his thigh with an awl.

They were not taught,

but toiled hard of their own accord.

如囊螢，如映雪。家雖貧，學不綴。

Then we have one who put fireflies in a bag.

and again another who used the white glare from snow.

Although their families were poor,

these men studied unceasingly.

如負薪，如掛角。身雖勞，猶苦卓。

Again, there was one who carried fuel,

and another who used horns as pegs.

Although they toiled with their bodies,

they were nevertheless remarkable for their application.

71-75 蘇老泉

蘇老泉，二十七。始發憤，讀書籍。

Su Lao-Quan,

at the age of twenty-seven,

at last began to show his energy

and devote himself to the study of books.

彼既老，猶悔遲。爾小生，宜早思。

Then when already past the age,

he deeply regretted his delay.

You little boys

should take thought betimes.

若梁灝，八十二。對大廷，魁多士。

Then there were Liang Hao,

who at the age of eighty-two,

made his replies in the great hall,

and came out first among many scholars.

彼既成，眾稱異。爾小生，宜立誌。

When thus late he had succeeded,

all men pronounced him a prodigy.

You little boys

should make up your minds to work.

瑩八歲，能詠詩。泌七歲，能賦碁。

Ying, at eight years of age,

could compose poetry.

Bi, at seven years of age,

could make an epigram on wei-qi.

76-80 彼穎悟

彼穎悟，人稱奇。爾幼學，當效之。

These youths were quick of apprehension,

and people declared them to be prodigies.

You young learners

ought to imitate them.

蔡文姬，能辨琴。謝道韞，能詠吟。

Cai Wen-ji,

was able to judge from the sound of a psaltery.

Xie Dao-yun,

was able to compose verses.

彼女子，且聰敏。爾男子，當自警。

They were only girls,

yet they were quick and clever.

You boys

ought to rouse yourselves.

唐劉晏，方七歲。舉神童，作正字。

Liu Yan of the Tang dynasty,

when only seven years of age,

was ranked as an "inspired child,"

and was appointed a Corrector of Texts.

彼雖幼，身己仕。爾幼學，勉而緻。有為者，亦若是。

He, although a child,

was already in an official post.

You young learners

strive to bring about a like result.

Those who work

will also succeed as he did.

81-86 犬守夜

犬守夜，雞司晨。苟不學，曷為人。

The dog keeps guard by night;

the cock proclaims the dawn.

If foolishly you do not study,

how can you become men?

蠶吐絲，蜂釀蜜。人不學，不如物。

The silkworm produces silk,

the bee makes honey.

If a man does not learn,

he is not equal to the brutes

幼而學，壯而行。上緻君，下澤民。

Learn while young,

and when grown up apply what you have learnt;

influencing the sovereign above;

benefiting the people below.

揚名聲，顯父母。光於前，裕於後。

Make a name for yourselves,

and glorify your father and mother,

shed lustre on your ancestors,

enrich your posterity.

人遺子，金滿嬴。我教子，惟一經。

Men bequeath to their children

coffers of gold;

I teach you children

only this one book.

勤有功，戲無益。戒之哉，宜勉力。

Diligence has its reward;

play has no advantages.

Oh, be on your guard,

and put forth your strength.

Classical Chinese Quick Study Guide

Classical Chinese 文言文, also known as Literary Chinese. While literary Chinese has been used for approximately 2,500 years, Classical Chinese "classic texts" were written from 5th century BC to 2nd century AD. This period roughly coincides from the end of the Spring and Autumn period through the end of the Han Dynasty. This unique form of Chinese comes from a long tradition of written Chinese, and does not correspond to spoken Chinese. In fact, many believe that Classical Chinese was never spoken at all, believing it was strictly a written form of communication. This tradition of formal Classical Chinese, similar to Latin in the West, is no longer widely used, being replaced with written vernacular modern Chinese. However, the rich heritage of Classical Chinese texts continue to influence the world with some of the greatest classic writing the world has produced.

Chinese speakers with at least a middle or high school education can read and interact with basic Classical Chinese. This is because it is part of the middle school and high school curriculum in China, and also tested in the critically important college entrance exam. Many of the classical texts continue to hold very strong cultural influence in China.

Characteristics of Classical Chinese
Concise and compact

Classical Chinese is generally more concise and compact than modern Chinese. A different vocabulary and set of unique characters is used. In some cases, Classical Chinese may use half the number of characters as modern Chinese to relay the same amount of information.

One syllable words

While modern Chinese utilizes two syllable words, Classical Chinese uses mostly one syllable words.

More pronouns

Classical Chinese has more pronouns than modern Chinese. This includes more pronouns for honorific situations and different grammatical uses.

Implied omission

Classical Chinese often drops subjects, verbs and objects that are implied or not necessary.

Words not restricted to set parts of speech

Words in Classical Chinese are not restricted to set parts of speech. A given word can act as a verb, adjective or a noun in different sentences.

More particles

Classical Chinese utilizes many particles for sentence endings and questions.

Reversed Word Order

Multiple character words in Classical Chinese can often reverse the order, retaining the meaning regardless of the reversal of the characters. For example, the word 饶恕 (ráoshù, "to forgive") may easily appear as 恕饶.

Most Important Chinese Classical Texts

The most important and culturally influential Chinese classical texts include the texts from Confucianism, Daoism, Mohism, Legalism, Military, Chinese history and poetry. From these categories, 9 specific books in particular were used as the center of the Imperial Examination educational system. These books have come to be known as the "Five Classics" and the "Four Books".

Five Classics:

1. 易经 I Ching, or Book of Changes. A divination manual for folk religion and fortunes.
2. 诗经 Classic of Poetry, collection of classic poems, songs, festival songs and eulogies.
3. 礼经 Classic of Rites
4. 尚书 Classic of History, history and speeches from rulers of the early Zhou period.
5. 春秋 Spring and Autumn Annals, historical records from Confucius' native state.

Four Books:

1. 论域 Analects of Confucius, teachings of Confucius written by his disciples.
2. 孟子 Mencius, political dialogues of the philosopher Mencius.
3. 中庸 Doctrine of the Mean, Confucian teaching from the Classic of Rites

4. 大学 Great Learning, Confucian teaching from the Classic of Rites

Other Major Classical Texts:

1. 道德经 Dao De Jing, primary Daoist philosophical text
2. 庄子 Zhuangzi, Daoist philosopher's teachings
3. 孙子兵法 The Art of War, military science by Sun Tzu
4. 唐诗 300 Tang Poems, classic collection of Tang Poetry
5. 列子 Liezi, Daoist philosopher's teachings

100 Most Frequent Classical Chinese Characters

1   之   zhi1   (literary equivalent of)/(subor. part.)/him/her/it

2   不   bu4/bu2   (negative prefix)/not/no

3   一   yi1   one/1/single/a(n)

4   人   ren2   man/person/people

5   以   yi3   to use/according to/so as to/in order to/by/with/because/Israel (abbrev.)

6   有   you3   to have/there is/there are/to exist/to be

7   了   le/liao3/liao4 (modal particle intensifying preceding clause)/(completed action marker), to know/to understand/to know, clear, look afar from a high place

8   为   wei2/wei4   act as/take...to be/to be/to do/to serve as/to become, because of/for/to

9   道   dao4   direction/way/method/road/path/principle/truth/reason/skill/method/Tao (of Taoism)/a measure word/to say/to speak/to talk

10   是   shi4   is/are/am/yes/to be

11 子 zi3/zi 11 p.m.-1 a.m./1st earthly branch/child/midnight/son/child/seed/egg/small thing, (noun suff.)

12 的 de/di2/di4 (possessive particle)/of, really and truly, aim/clear

13 来 lai2 to come

14 大 da4/dai4 big/huge/large/major/great/wide/deep/oldest/eldest, doctor

15 也 ye3 also/too

16 十 shi2 ten/10

17 其 qi2 his/her/its/theirs/that/such/it (refers to sth preceding it)

18 上 shang4 on/on top/upon/first (of two parts)/previous or last (week, etc.)/upper/higher/above/previous/to climb/to go into/above/to go up

19 二 er4 two/2

20 而 er2 and/as well as/but (not)/yet (not)/(shows causal relation)/(shows change of state)/(shows contrast)

21   中   zhong1/zhong4
within/among/in/middle/center/while   (doing sth)/during/China/Chinese, hit (the mark)

22   曰   yue1   to speak/to say

23   下   xia4   under/second (of two parts)/next (week, etc.)/lower/below/underneath/down(wards)/to decline/to go down/latter

24   于   yu2   (surname), in/at/to/from/by/than/out of

25   三   san1   three/3

26   得   de2/de/dei3
obtain/get/gain/proper/suitable/proud/contented/allow/permit/ready/finished, a sentence particle used after a verb to show effect/degree or possibility, to have to/must/ought to/to need to

27   在   zai4   (located) at/in/exist

28   年   nian2   year

29   我   wo3   I/me/myself

30   他   ta1   he/him

31   王   wang2 king/Wang (proper name)

32   说   shui4/shuo1   persuade (politically), to speak/to say

33   事   shi4   matter/thing/item/work/affair

34   见   jian4/xian4   to see/to meet/to appear (to be sth)/to interview, appear

35   将   jiang1/jiang4 (will, shall, "future tense")/ready/prepared/to get/to use, a general

36   者   zhe3   -ist, -er (person)/person (who does sth)

37   去   qu4   to go/to leave/to remove

38   日   ri4   Japan/day/sun/date/day of the month

39   天   tian1   day/sky/heaven

40   州   zhou1 (United States) state/province/sub-prefecture

41   出   chu1   to go out/to come out/to occur/to produce/to go beyond/to rise/to put forth/to occur/to happen/(a measure word for dramas, plays, or operas)

42   后   hou4   empress/queen/surname, back/behind/rear/afterwards/after/later

43   又   you4   (once) again/also/both... and.../again

44   自   zi4   from/self/oneself/since

45   此   ci3   this/these

46   个   ge4   (a measure word)/individual

47   时   shi2
o'clock/time/when/hour/season/period

48   无   wu2   -less/not to have/no/none/not/to
lack/un-

49   军   1-Jun   army/military/arms

50   太   tai4   highest/greatest/too
(much)/very/extremely

51   这   zhe4/zhei4   this/these,
this/these/(sometimes used before a measure word,
especially in Beijing)

52   与   yu2/yu3/yu4   (interrog.   part.),   and/to
give/together with, take part in

53   月   yue4   moon/month

54   所   suo3   actually/place

55   家   jia1   furniture/tool,   -ist/-er/-
ian/home/family/a person engaged in a certain art or
profession

56   如   ru2   as (if)/such as

57   知   zhi1   to know/to be aware

58　　你　　ni3　　you

59　　里　　li3　　inside/internal/interior, village/within/inside, Chinese mile/neighborhood/li, a Chinese unit of length = one-half kilometer/hometown

60　　公　　gong1 just/honorable (designation)/public/common

61　　行　　hang2/xing2/xing4　　a row/profession/professional,　　all right/capable/competent/OK/okay/to　　go/to　　do/to travel/temporary/to walk/to go/will do, behavior/conduct

62　　可　　ke3　　can/may/able　　to/certain(ly)/to suit/(particle used for emphasis)

63　　使　　shi3　　to　make/to　cause/to　enable/to use/to employ/messenger

64　　到　　dao4　　to (a place)/until (a time)/up to/to go/to arrive

65　　四　　si4　　four/4

66　　至　　zhi4　　arrive/most/to/until

67　　五　　wu3　　five/5

68　　那　　na3/na4/nei4 how/which,　　that/those, that/those/(sometimes used before a measure word, especially in Beijing)

69   官   guan1   official/government

70   书   shu1   book/letter

71   生   sheng1 to be born/to give birth/life/to grow

72   小   xiao3   small/tiny/few/young

73   言   yan2   to speak/to say/talk/word

74   何   he2   carry/what/how/why/which

75   相   xiang1/xiang4 each other/one another/mutually, appearance/portrait/picture

76   兵   bing1   soldiers/a force/an army/weapons/arms/military/warlike

77   今   jin1
      today/modern/present/current/this/now

78   都   dou1/du1   all/both (if two things are involved)/entirely   (due   to)each/even/already, (surname)/metropolis/capital city

79   南   nan2   south

80   山   shan1   mountain/hill

81   就   jiu4   at   once/then/right away/only/(emphasis)/to approach/to move towards/to undertake

82   只   qi2/zhi1/zhi3   earth-spirit/peace,   (a measure   word,   for   birds   and   some   animals, etc.)/single/only, M for one of a pair, only/merely/just/but, but/only

83   正   zheng1/zheng4   Chinese 1st month of year, just (right)/main/upright/straight/correct/principle

84   前   qian2   before/in front/ago/former/previous/earlier/front

85   明   ming2   clear/bright/to understand/next/the Ming dynasty

86   东   dong1   east

87   着   zhao1/zhao2/zhe/zhu4/zhuo2   catch/receive/suffer, part. indicates the successful result of a verb/to touch/to come in contact with/to feel/to be affected by/to catch fire/to fall asleep/to burn, -ing part. (indicates an action in progress)/part. coverb-forming after some verbs, to make known/to show/to prove/to write/book/outstanding, to wear (clothes)/to contact/to use/to apply

88   门   men2   opening/door/gate/doorway/gateway/valve/switch/way to do something/knack/family/house/(religious) sect/school (of thought)/class/category/phylum or division (taxonomy)

89   帝   di4   emperor

90　等　deng3 class/rank/grade/equal　to/same as/wait for/await/et cetera/and so on

91　文　wen2
language/culture/writing/formal/literary

92　国　guo2　country/state/nation

93　百　bai3　hundred

94　西　xi1　west

95　心　xin1　heart/mind

96　安　an1　content/calm/still/quiet/to pacify/peace

97　然　ran2　correct/right/so/thus/like this/-ly

98　要　yao1/yao4　demand/ask/request/coerce, important/vital/to want/to be going to/must

99　好　hao3/hao4　good/well, be fond of

100　入　ru4　to enter

Made in the USA
Lexington, KY
18 May 2019